Joseph McCarthy: The Controversial Life and Career of 20th Century America's Most Notorious Senator

By Charles River Editors

About Charles River Editors

Charles River Editors provides superior editing and original writing services across the digital publishing industry, with the expertise to create digital content for publishers across a vast range of subject matter. In addition to providing original digital content for third party publishers, we also republish civilization's greatest literary works, bringing them to new generations of readers via ebooks.

Sign up here to receive updates about free books as we publish them, and visit Our Kindle Author Page to browse today's free promotions and our most recently published Kindle titles.

Introduction

Joseph McCarthy (1908-1957)

"Today we are engaged in a final, all-out battle between communistic atheism and Christianity. The modern champions of communism have selected this as the time, and ladies and gentlemen, the chips are down — they are truly down." – Joseph McCarthy

"I will not get in the gutter with that guy." – President Dwight D. Eisenhower

Shortly after World War II, Congress' House Committee on Un-American Activities began investigating Americans across the country for suspected ties to Communism. The most famous victims of these witch hunts were Hollywood actors, such as Charlie Chaplin, whose "Un-American activity" was being neutral at the beginning of World War II. However, Elizabeth Bentley, a former communist, notified the Committee about one suspected spy ring and named several names, including Alger Hiss. Hiss was a prominent New Dealer who served on the American delegation to the San Francisco Conference that established the United Nations, and he strongly denied being a Communist, much less a spy. A former communist named Whittaker Chambers also accused Hiss of being in his Communist group, and again Hiss denied it.

Eventually, Hiss was convicted of perjury when it was shown he had been a member of the Communist party in the mid-1930s, but in spite of the FBI's best efforts, its special agents never developed definitive proof that Hiss was a spy. Controversy swirled for decades over the charges, and for many the Hiss case was proof of Cold War anti-Communist hysteria.

Another factor was the disrepute the Red Scare fell into because of the antics of Wisconsin Senator Joseph McCarthy. McCarthy had made waves in 1950 by telling the Republican Women's Club in Wheeling, West Virginia that he had a list of dozens of known Communists working in the State Department. The political theater helped Senator McCarthy become the most prominent anti-Communist crusader in the government, and the Rosenberg case only further emboldened him. McCarthy continued to claim he held evidence suggesting Communist infiltration throughout the government, but anytime he was pressed to produce his evidence, McCarthy would not name names. Instead, he'd accuse those who questioned his evidence of being Communists themselves.

McCarthy's rise made it possible for him to continue lobbing accusations against people, but the Senator finally met his match when he went after the Army. As chairman of the Senate Committee on Government Operations, McCarthy summoned decorated World War II veterans and challenged their loyalty, and when he openly suggested World War II hero Brigadier General Ralph W. Zwicker was a Communist during one hearing, the military had enough. In April 1954, the committee hearings were widely televised, and Americans watched Army members demand that McCarthy name names and provide evidence. On June 9, 1954, McCarthy was humiliated by the Army's legal representative, Joseph Nye Welch, who repeatedly demanded that McCarthy produce the list of alleged Communists in the U.S. Army. As McCarthy tried to wiggle out of the challenge, he finally named Fred Fisher, who had been affiliated with the National Lawyers Guild during law school, an organization that FBI Director J. Edgar Hoover attempted to have the Attorney General designate as a Communist front. Enraged, Welch responded, "Until this moment, Senator, I think I have never really gauged your cruelty or your recklessness. Fred Fisher is a young man who went to the Harvard Law School and came into my firm and is starting what looks to be a brilliant career with us...We know he belonged to the Lawyers Guild. Let us not assassinate this lad further, Senator. You've done enough. Have you no sense of decency, sir? At long last, have you left no sense of decency?" Welch received an ovation from the gallery, and McCarthy had been publicly and permanently repudiated. He would be censured by Congress, and he would die just a few years later.

Though anti-Communist sentiment in the 1950s is often derisively dismissed as McCarthyism, there was some basis for the era's fears. The Communist Party in the United States was funded by the Soviet Union; its leaders were paid by the Soviets, and several were agents of the Soviet intelligence apparatus. During the 1930s, the Party had gained members who believed that the capitalist system was dying and the future lay with Communism, and those members also believed that the Communists were the only effective bulwark against Hitler and the rise of fascism. However, after the signing of the Soviet-German Non-Aggression Pact in 1939, the

Communist Party lost members and never recovered the numbers it had in the mid-1930s. Still, as a small elite group, able to place individuals in positions of power, they did present a potential threat to the security of the country, and there were several spy rings operating in America at the time.

Joseph McCarthy: The Controversial Life and Career of 20th Century America's Most Notorious Senator examines the life and career of the controversial Senator. Along with pictures of important people, places, and events, you will learn about McCarthy like never before, in no time at all.

Joseph McCarthy: The Controversial Life and Career of 20th Century America's Most Notorious Senator

About Charles River Editors

Introduction

  Chapter 1: Someone Had to Do the Job

  Chapter 2: How to Arouse the Public to the Danger

  Chapter 3: The Tydings Committee

  Chapter 4: Eisenhower's Hands Are Also Tied

  Chapter 5: Disloyal Elements

  Chapter 6: Guilty of Hoodwinking the American Public

  Chapter 7: Bleed Them

  Online Resources

  Bibliography

Chapter 1: Someone Had to Do the Job

"As I walked toward the hearing room, many things crossed my mind. For example, in a few seconds I relived the first trip which I had taken in the rear seat of an SBD to dive bomb Japanese anti-aircraft on the then southern anchor of the chain of Japanese Pacific defenses at Kahili on the southern tip of Bougainville. Apparently I had complained too much about the lack of photo coverage for our dive and torpedo bombing strikes for I suddenly found myself the Pacific's most reluctant 'volunteer' cameraman in the rear seat of a dive bomber. As we flew over the Japanese airfield on Ballale island that morning, a few minutes before our break-off for the dive through Kahili's anti-aircraft fire, there crossed my mind the thought: 'McCarthy, why are you here? Why isn't it someone else? Why did you have to be the one who objected so much to the bad photo coverage?' But then I remembered the next thought which I had as my pilot — I believe it was little Johnny Morton — cracked his flaps and I saw the red undercover as the dive bombing brakes opened up. My thought was: 'Hell, someone had to do the job. It might as well be me.'" – Joseph McCarthy, *McCarthyism: The Fight for America* (1952)

There are few people in 20th century American history who are as maligned today as Joseph McCarthy. Born on November 14, 1908, he came of age in a time of war, political and social upheaval, and more war. Whatever else might be said about him, it seems that his goal during most of his adult life was to preserve the country he loved from being overturned during the storms that were swirling about it. While his techniques were at the very least questionable and his personality undoubtedly obsessive, it is only fair to give him at least a little credit for having good intentions, at least initially.

Those intentions were first formed on a farm outside Grand Chute, Wisconsin, where he was born the fifth of seven children. He was the son of Bridget and Timothy McCarthy, both of whom raised him with the kind of love for America that immigrants and their children often have. At 14, he had to drop out of school to help on the farm, and when he was 19, he left home and moved to nearby Manawa. A friend later recalled, "Joe was steamed up when he came to Manawa. I never saw anybody so steamed up. He just couldn't ever relax; he worked at everything he did. He was pushing all the time."

The pushing culminated in a surprising feat of ambition and determination when McCarthy returned to school at the age of 20 and graduated within just a year. He then moved on to Marquette University, where he earned a Law Degree. Charles Curran, whom he beat out for class president, remembered him fondly: "My father died in 1933 while I was in school. Just before the funeral Joe drove all the way out to our house in an old Model A he'd borrowed. He cut classes, left his job, and borrowed money to get there. He did that for me, and he'll always be my friend."

McCarthy in 1930

McCarthy entered politics for the first time in 1936, the year he ran for district attorney of Shawano, Wisconsin. He lost that election, but he was elected as a Circuit Judge for the Wisconsin's 10th District in 1939. Once on the bench, he developed a reputation for the speed with which he worked, which came as a welcome relief to many since he inherited quite a backlog of cases. He was also popular for expediting divorce cases while at the same time showing interest in the impact his decision would have on the children involved.

He was able to work even faster when there were no children involved, leading one divorcee, Chester Roberts, to note, "My wife and her lawyer headed for Marinette to get the divorce before Judge Harold Murphy. It was perfectly all right with me; the sooner they got it over with the better. On the way, they went through Appleton and happened to bump into Joe. Next thing I know, Joe had settled the whole mess."

As it turned out, Chester Roberts was no ordinary Joe; in fact, he was the chairman of the Milwaukee County Young Republicans, so when McCarthy worked on his divorce in September 1946, it led the *Milwaukee Journal* to complain, "It was quick, it was quiet, it was without publicity. And no doubt it was legal. ... Is Wisconsin justice to be used to accommodate political supporters of a presiding judge? Are Wisconsin courts the place in which to settle political debts? … Judge McCarthy, whose burning ambition for political advancement is accompanied by an astonishing disregard for things ethical and traditional, is doing serious injury to the judiciary of this state." The *Journal* also noted that McCarthy was running for the U.S. Senate in 1946 despite Wisconsin law prohibiting sitting judges from running for elected office. In spite of this and other criticisms, very few of McCarthy's decisions were ever overturned.

Even before he started courting controversy in Wisconsin, McCarthy's judicial career was interrupted by World War II. In 1942, at the age of 33, he enlisted in the United States Marine Corps, and upon completing basic training, he was made a second lieutenant and assigned as an intelligence briefing officer for a squadron of dive bombers in the Solomon Islands. Like many other veterans, his war record would certainly help his career, and it seems that political ambition was on his mind even during combat. Lieutenant P.T. Kimball relayed one story about their service together: "I remember a day when we were both at Munda when Joe's squadron was flying a 'milk run' to Bougainville. The job was bombing runways on old airfields to make sure the Japs didn't try to come back. It was dull duty, and the bored fliers decided to see how many flights they could make in a day. McCarthy, like other ground officers, joined in the fun to ride as a tail gunner. As public relations officer, I wrote a form story about 'the record-breaking day of bombing,' filled in the names of the men involved and sent them along slugged 'from an advance Marine base.' I forgot the whole thing till McCarthy came around with a handful of clippings from Wisconsin papers. This is worth 50,000 votes to me,' McCarthy said. 'Come, have a drink on it.'"

McCarthy in his uniform

McCarthy served as a gunner observer on real combat missions before being discharged in 1945 with a rank of Captain and the nickname "Tail-Gunner Joe." He was also given the following citation: "For meritorious and efficient performance of duty as an observer and rear gunner of a dive bomber attached to a Marine scout bombing squadron operating in the Solomon Islands area from September 1 to December 31, 1943. He participated in a large number of combat missions, and in addition to his regular duties, acted as aerial photographer. He obtained excellent photographs of enemy gun positions, despite intense anti-aircraft fire, thereby gaining valuable information which contributed materially to the success of subsequent strikes in the area. Although suffering from a severe leg injury, he refused to be hospitalized and continued to carry out his duties as Intelligence Officer in a highly efficient manner. His courageous devotion to duty was in keeping with the highest traditions of the naval service."

Furthermore, McCarthy came back from the war even wealthier than he had been thanks to a number of prudent investments he made during the war. Roy Cohn, who would go on to become a member of McCarthy's investigating committee, wrote that McCarthy "made small investments all the time, but he played around the way the average man would play gin rummy. He would come up with a 'sensational' idea upon which he would proceed to place a small bet in the form of an investment. Then he'd forget about it. He dabbled in the stock and commodities markets. He was in and out all the time I knew him; it was a form of relaxation, without much common sense or judgment or even real interest."

While he was still in the Pacific, McCarthy was recruited by Wisconsin Republicans to run for the U.S. Senate. He replied to their request, "Some time ago I received your letter in which you, in behalf of the committee, ask whether I would be willing to serve if elected to the U.S. Senate. This is the first opportunity I have had to answer, but I have given the matter serious consideration. My answer is yes. You understand, of course, that I shall take no part in the campaign. In fact, I do not even expect to be in the United States before the election, and I cannot, because of military regulations, discuss political issues. But I do have a program, and this I will submit to the people of Wisconsin as soon as the time permits. I must, of necessity, leave this campaign to my friends and the voters of Wisconsin, because I shall continue on out here, doing to the best of my ability those tasks assigned to me."

By the time the election rolled around, he was back stateside, but he was defeated. He then successfully ran unopposed for his judicial position, a post he held while he prepared to make a more serious run for the Senate in 1946. He quickly went on the offensive against the 52 year old incumbent, Robert M. La Follette, Jr., criticizing him for not fighting in the war and accusing him of war profiteering. One of McCarthy's advertisements read, "JOE MC CARTHY WAS A TAIL GUNNER in World War II. When the war began Joe had a soft job as a Judge at EIGHT GRAND a year. He was EXEMPT from military duty. He resigned his job to enlist as a PRIVATE in the MARINES. He fought on LAND and in the AIR all through the Pacific. He and millions of other guys kept you from talking Japanese. TODAY JOE MCCARTHY IS HOME. He wants to SERVE America in the SENATE. Yes, folks, CONGRESS NEEDS A TAIL GUNNER. Now, when Washington is in confusion, when BUREAUCRATS are seeking to perpetuate themselves FOREVER upon the American way of life, AMERICA NEEDS FIGHTING MEN. These men who fought upon foreign soil to SAVE AMERICA have earned the right to SERVE AMERICA in times of peace."

La Follette, Jr.

His strategy worked, and McCarthy won the Republican nomination. He kept up his assault during the general election, accusing his opponent of being soft on Communism and alleging in one ad, "Some of the Democratic candidates for high offices in the government have been repudiated by the party because they have been proven to have Communist backgrounds and Communist ways of thinking. Others have been touched with suspicion, but the proof is lacking. Joseph R. McCarthy is 100 percent American in thought and deed. No one can say that he believes in any foreign isms that have plagued the Democratic Party throughout their reign. This is America. Let's have Americans in the government."

Once again, this strategy paid off. In November 1946, Joseph McCarthy became the junior Senator from the State of Wisconsin.

Chapter 2: How to Arouse the Public to the Danger

"I have often wondered how the extremely busy Secretary of the Navy discovered that a freshman Senator had arrived in town and why he took so much time out to discuss the problems which, were so deeply disturbing him. More than an equal number of times I have thanked God that he did. ... When I took on my duties as a Senator, I discovered that certain outstanding Senators and Congressmen for years had been intelligently trying to alert the American people. They belonged to both parties. Unfortunately, when they clearly and intelligently presented a picture of incompetence or treason which should have commanded banner headlines in every newspaper, the story was found, if at all, hidden in want-ad space and type. I witnessed the frustration of those honest, intelligent, loyal Americans who were attempting to expose our suicidal foreign policy. Day after day I came into contact with convincing evidence of treason. Obviously, unless the public was aroused, the downward course upon which we were embarked would continue and at an accelerated pace. But how to arouse the public to the danger before it was too late?" – Joseph McCarthy, *McCarthyism: The Fight for America* (1952)

Joe McCarthy had successfully run a campaign for the Senate, but it soon seemed that he was not up to the actual job itself. While he could be quite charming with those outside the halls of Congress, his fellow Senators found him to be irritating and hot-tempered. He tried to make his name in a number of areas, first by working on labor unions and then price controls, and ironically, he was considered moderate in his views, going so far as to criticize the way in which German prisoners of war had been treated and calling for the death sentences of a number of convicted Nazi war criminals to be commuted. Still, he was unable to make those all-important connections with the press, who voted him "the worst U.S. senator" then in office.

As a new decade dawned, everything changed in the blink of an eye. On February 9, 1950, McCarthy gave a speech that would change the trajectory of his career and shape the political climate of 1950s America. It should not have been a big speech; in fact, it was given before a small group of housewives who were members of the Republican Women's Club of Wheeling, West Virginia. While no audio recording of the speech was made at the time, McCarthy later read a version of it into the Congressional Record.

After making a few pleasant opening remarks, he shocked his audience by proclaiming, "The great difference between our western Christian world and the atheistic Communist world is not political, gentlemen, it is moral. For instance, the Marxian idea of confiscating the land and factories and running the entire economy as a single enterprise is momentous. Likewise, Lenin's invention of the one-party police state as a way to make Marx's idea work is hardly less momentous. Stalin's resolute putting across of these two ideas, of course, did much to divide the world. With only these differences, however, the east and the west could most certainly still live in peace. The real, basic difference, however, lies in the religion of immoralism . . . invented by Marx, preached feverishly by Lenin, and carried to unimaginable extremes by Stalin. This religion of immoralism, if the Red half of the world triumphs—and well it may, gentlemen—this religion of immoralism will more deeply wound and damage mankind than any conceivable economic or political system. Karl Marx dismissed God as a hoax, and Lenin and Stalin have added in clear-cut, unmistakable language their resolve that no nation, no people who believe in a god, can exist side by side with their communistic state. Karl Marx, for example, expelled people from his Communist Party for mentioning such things as love, justice, humanity or morality. He called this 'soulful ravings' and 'sloppy sentimentality.'"

Having begun by playing up Communism's threat to general morality, he became even more specific, telling the churchgoing ladies that Communism was a threat to the Christian faith itself. "Today we are engaged in a final, all-out battle between communistic atheism and Christianity. The modern champions of communism have selected this as the time, and ladies and gentlemen, the chips are down—they are truly down. Lest there be any doubt that the time has been chosen, let us go directly to the leader of communism today—Joseph Stalin. Here is what he said—not back in 1928, not before the war, not during the war—but 2 years after the last war was ended: 'To think that the Communist revolution can be carried out peacefully, within the framework of a Christian democracy, means one has either gone out of one's mind and lost all normal understanding, or has grossly and openly repudiated the Communist revolution.'

McCarthy knew some in the audience might have assumed that Communists were only in Russia and couldn't hurt America, and for that, he had a ready response: "Six years ago, . . . there was within the Soviet orbit, 180,000,000 people. Lined up on the antitotalitarian side there were in the world at that time, roughly 1,625,000,000 people. Today, only six years later, there are 800,000,000 people under the absolute domination of Soviet Russia—an increase of over 400 percent. On our side, the figure has shrunk to around 500,000,000. In other words, in less than six years, the odds have changed from 9 to 1 in our favor to 8 to 5 against us. This indicates the swiftness of the tempo of Communist victories and American defeats in the cold war. As one of our outstanding historical figures once said, 'When a great democracy is destroyed, it will not be from enemies from without, but rather because of enemies from within.' ... The reason why we find ourselves in a position of impotency is not because our only powerful potential enemy has sent men to invade our shores . . . but rather because of the traitorous actions of those who have been treated so well by this Nation. It has not been the less fortunate, or members of minority groups who have been traitorous to this Nation, but rather those who have had all the benefits that the wealthiest Nation on earth has had to offer . . . the finest homes, the finest college education and the finest jobs in government we can give. This is glaringly true in the State Department. There the bright young men who are born with silver spoons in their mouths are the ones who have been most traitorous... This, ladies and gentlemen, gives you somewhat of a picture of the type of individuals who have been helping to shape our foreign policy. In my opinion the State Department, which is one of the most important government departments, is thoroughly infested with Communists. I have in my hand 57 cases of Individuals who would appear to be either card carrying members or certainly loyal to the Communist Party, but who nevertheless are still helping to shape our foreign policy. ... This brings us down to the case of one Alger Hiss who is important not as an individual any more, but rather because he is so representative of a group in the State Department. It is unnecessary to go over the sordid events showing how he sold out the Nation which had given him so much. Those are rather fresh in all of our minds."

Hiss

Then came the final blow, the culmination of his speech and the beginning of his crusade. Waving a paper for all to see, he announced, "I have here in my hand a list of … names that were made known to the Secretary of State as being members of the Communist Party and who nevertheless are still working and shaping policy in the State Department. … As you know, very recently the Secretary of State proclaimed his loyalty to a man guilty of what has always been considered as the most abominable of all crimes—being a traitor to the people who gave him a position of great trust—high treason. … He has lighted the spark which is resulting in a moral uprising and will end only when the whole sorry mess of twisted, warped thinkers are swept from the national scene so that we may have a new birth of honesty and decency in government."

Once back in Washington, McCarthy wasted no time in following up on his remarks. Two days later, on February 11, 1950, he sent a letter to President Harry Truman in which he reiterated his remarks and reminded him, "You will recall that you personally appointed a board to screen State Department employees for the purpose of weeding out fellow travelers—men whom the board considered dangerous to the security of this Nation. Your board did a painstaking job, and named hundreds which had been listed as dangerous to the security of the Nation, because of communistic connections." He then called on Truman to "pick up your phone and ask Mr. [Dean] Acheson how many of those whom your board had labeled as dangerous Communists he failed to discharge." Then, in an almost threatening tone, he pointed out that Truman had "signed an order forbidding the State Department's giving any information in regard to the disloyalty or the communistic connections of anyone in that Department to the Congress."

Of course, McCarthy also offered a solution to correct this situation:

> "Despite this State Department black-out, we have been able to compile a list of 57 Communists in the State Department. This list is available to you but you can get a much longer list by ordering Secretary Acheson to give you a list of those whom your own board listed as being disloyal and who are still working in the State Department. I believe the following is the minimum which can be expected of you in this case.
>
> 1. That you demand that Acheson give you and the proper congressional committee the names and a complete report on all of those who were placed in the Department by Alger Hiss, and all of those still working in the State Department who were listed by your board as bad security risks because of their communistic connections.
>
> 2. That you promptly revoke the order in which you provided under no circumstances could a congressional committee obtain any information or help in exposing Communists."

He concluded forcefully, "Failure on your part will label the Democratic Party of being the bedfellow of international communism. Certainly this label is not deserved by the hundreds of thousands of loyal American Democrats throughout the Nation, and by the sizable number of able loyal Democrats in both the Senate and the House."

Acheson

During his presidency, Truman had tried to play down public fears, and privately he despised McCarthy. In 1947, the president assured Americans, "I am not worried about the Communist Party taking over the Government of the United States, but I am against a person, whose loyalty is not to the Government of the United States, holding a Government job. They are entirely different things. I am not worried about this country ever going Communist. We have too much sense for that."

During one of his last official functions as President, Truman delivered an address at the National Archives in which he decried the hysteria and identified the true threat to the country's democracy:

"Of course, there are dangers in religious freedom and freedom of opinion. But to deny these rights is worse than dangerous, it is absolutely fatal to liberty. The external threat to liberty should not drive us into suppressing liberty at home. Those who want the Government to regulate matters of the mind and spirit are like men who are so afraid of being murdered that they commit suicide to avoid assassination.

All freedom-loving nations, not the United States alone, are facing a stern challenge from the Communist tyranny. In the circumstances, alarm is justified. The man who isn't alarmed simply doesn't understand the situation — or he is crazy. But alarm is one thing, and hysteria is another. Hysteria impels people to destroy the very thing they are struggling to preserve.

Invasion and conquest by Communist armies would be a horror beyond our capacity to imagine. But invasion and conquest by Communist ideas of right and wrong would be just as bad.

For us to embrace the methods and morals of communism in order to defeat Communist aggression would be a moral disaster worse than any physical catastrophe. If that should come to pass, then the Constitution and the Declaration would be utterly dead and what we are doing today would be the gloomiest burial in the history of the world."

After the hysteria of McCarthyism waned, Truman would defiantly assert in 1960, "I've said many a time that I think the Un-American Activities Committee in the House of Representatives was the most un-American thing in America!"

Chapter 3: The Tydings Committee

"The Senate had authorized the Tydings Committee to investigate Communist infiltration of government. The Senate had given that committee power, investigators, and money to run down every lead on Communists in government which I gave them. Today, March 8, 1950, my task was to give the committee the leads which would be a basis for their investigation…Over two weeks had elapsed since my Senate speech which had forced the creation of the Tydings Committee. Already it had become very apparent that this was to be no ordinary investigation. It was to be a contest between a lone Senator and all the vast power of the federal bureaucracy pinpointed in and backing up the Tydings Committee. The picture of treason which I carried in my briefcase to that Caucus room was to shock the nation and occupy the headlines until Truman declared war in Korea. But there was nothing new about this picture. The general pattern was known to every legislator in Washington, except those who deliberately blinded their eyes and closed their ears to the unpleasant truth." – Joseph McCarthy, *McCarthyism: The Fight for America* (1952)

Even McCarthy was surprised at the public reaction in favor of his speech, but unfortunately for his cause, the public outcry was accompanied by public scrutiny. Most importantly, people noticed that he changed the number of people he claimed were communists working for the State Department on several occasions when he and his speech came to national attention. In fact, it's still unknown whether he claimed to have a list of 205 names or 58 names in Wheeling.

Whatever the case, the numbers that McCarthy did use most likely came from a list compiled after the end of World War II by the House Appropriations Committee. A former FBI agent named Robert Lee found "incidents of inefficiencies" in the security reviews of 108 employees, and McCarthy successfully exaggerated the information on this list to his own ends. McCarthy's charges compelled the Senate to appoint a Subcommittee on the Investigation of Loyalty of State Department Employees, better known as the Tydings Committee, in February 1950. According to McCarthy, "The Tydings Committee was set up as a result of information which I gave the Senate about the Communist connections of a sizable number of present and past State Department employees. I gave the Senate a brief review of the files of 81 individuals who were then or had been closely connected with the State Department. At that time I informed the Senate that I did not have the staff, the power of subpoena, or the facilities to produce all of the available evidence against those individuals, but that the evidence which I had clearly indicated that many of them were either Communists or doing the work of the Communist Party. Others were marginal cases who might be able to prove their loyalty. The Senate thereupon voted unanimously that the Foreign Relations Committee should hold hearings. It ordered that committee to subpoena all of the files on those named by me. The Tydings Committee was given all the money, investigators, and power it needed to do the job."

Tydings

Led by Senator Millard Tydings, a Democrat from Maryland, the committee was tasked with conducting "a full and complete study and investigation as to whether persons who are disloyal to the United States are, or have been, employed by the Department of State". However, Tydings was determined to find nothing, and he once said of McCarthy, "Let me have him for three days in public hearings, and he'll never show his face in the Senate again." Democratic Senator Scott Lucas, the Senate Majority Leader at the time, admitted, "All we are trying to do is to give the Committee on Foreign Relations jurisdiction of the proposed investigation, rather than have the Committee on the Judiciary or the Committee on Expenditures in the Executive Departments, or some other committee immediately take jurisdiction…"

Lucas

Unfortunately for Tydings, McCarthy was more than his equal in front of an audience. Instead of continuing to make general accusations against a nameless crowd, McCarthy went after 9 State Department employees by name, telling the committee, "On the Senate floor I said that I would not divulge any names. I said I hoped any names that were divulged would be developed in executive session. Mr. Lucas, who is the leader of the majority party, demanded time after time on the Senate floor and publicly that I divulge names. I am now before the committee. In order to present the case I must give the names, otherwise I cannot intelligibly present it. If the committee desires to go into executive session, that is a decision that the committee and not I can make, but if I am to testify, I say it is impossible to do it without divulging names . . . I personally do not favor presenting names, no matter how conclusive the evidence is. The committee has called me this morning, and in order to intelligibly present this information I must give names. I think this should be in executive session. I think it would be better. However, I am here. The committee has voted to hold open sessions, so I shall proceed."

Among those he named was Dorothy Kenyon, a feminist and member of the United Nations Commission on the Status of Women. McCarthy claimed that he had evidence from two "reliable former members of the Communist party … [that] she had one job and one job only and that was to attach herself to a prominent individual... high in public life and try to influence the writings of that individual." Kenyon fought back hard, announcing, "I am not, and never have been, a supporter of, a member of, or a sympathizer with any organization known to me to be, or suspected by me, of being controlled or dominated by Communists." The committee agreed with her, and the charges against her were dismissed.

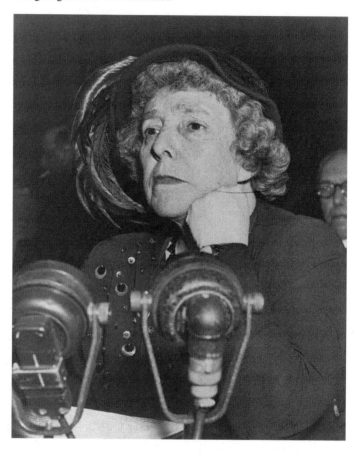

Kenyon testifying before Congress

McCarthy also attacked Owen Lattimore, a State Department expert on the Far East, whom he referred to as a "top Russian spy." McCarthy claimed that "13 different witnesses have testified under oath to Lattimore's Communist membership or party line activities." However, Truman stood by his man, and *The New York Times* reported on March 31, 1950, "The President paid a glowing tribute to Senator McCarthy's three major targets: Dean Acheson, Secretary of State; Philip C. Jessup, senior adviser to Mr. Acheson; and Owen Lattimore, one-time consultant to the State Department on Far Eastern Affairs ... 'You don't believe he is a spy?' asked a reporter, referring to Mr. McCarthy's charge that Mr. Lattimore was Russia's leading agent in this country.

Of course, he did not believe that, Mr. Truman replied with asperity. It was silly on the face of it and people recognized it, he said."

Lattimore and his wife

Between Truman's support and McCarthy's lack of evidence, the Tydings Committee had no problem clearing everyone accused, which was a relief to the Democrats in the Senate. Tydings called McCarthy's allegations a "fraud and a hoax [designed to]…confuse and divide the American people... to a degree far beyond the hopes of the Communists themselves".

Conversely, angry Republicans accused Tydings of "the most brazen whitewash of treasonable conspiracy in our history," and not surprisingly, McCarthy claimed that the committee had been formed to squelch his claims from the beginning: "The Tydings Committee was, of course, carefully selected to do the job which it finally did. At that time there was in existence a Special Senate Investigating Committee fully staffed with competent investigators which could have done the job. The Judiciary Committee, headed by a great American who is anti-Communist, Senator Pat McCarran, also could have done the job. But the Foreign Relations Committee was selected. …the committee was not formed to make a complete investigation but to prevent a real investigation."

McCarthy also attacked Truman and blamed him for the committee's failure to turn up more communists, complaining that "the President publicly announced that he would defy the Senate subpoena for the loyalty files, saying he would stand pat on his 1948 order instructing all government departments to refuse to let Congress look at loyalty records of Government employees. At the same time President Truman indicated that he would make available any files which would disprove Senator McCarthy's charges of Communist infiltration. In other words, if a file would prove that a man was guilty of treason or Communist activities, the Committee, according to Truman, could not see that file. If the file would prove that McCarthy was wrong then the file could be seen by the committee."

Chapter 4: Eisenhower's Hands Are Also Tied

"Those who have confidence in General Eisenhower as a great soldier should realize that Eisenhower's hands are also tied by the same crowd that has tied the hands of MacArthur in the East, and if good-natured Ike isn't careful, he is going to be taken for an awful ride. You know a good soldier does not have time to learn the ways of crooked, backroom diplomacy, and if he has spent enough time soldiering to be the good soldier that Eisenhower is, he cannot cope with unprincipled, crooked, clever diplomats. It is difficult for a soldier of integrity who has not had time off to study the ways of traitors to bring himself to believe that people in high positions could be actually disloyal to this nation. The Senate will recall that when the General appeared before the Joint Session of the Congress, he said he was unable to discuss the use of German manpower until the policies of the situation were cleared up by the diplomats. And for five years those diplomats have done nothing to clear up the situation." – Joseph McCarthy, *McCarthyism: The Fight for America* (1952)

Undeterred by the Tydings Committee, McCarthy continued devoting himself to trying to weed out Communists in the United States government. Much of his work focused on those known or suspected to be homosexual, and while this was no doubt at least somewhat motivated by his own bigotry, he claimed to have a practical concern for doing so. According to McCarthy, "One reason why sex deviates are considered by all intelligence agencies of the government to be security risks is that they are subject to blackmail. It is a known fact that espionage agents often have been successful in extorting information from them by threatening to expose their abnormal habits." To be fair, McCarthy wasn't the only one who thought this way; Roscoe Hillenkoetter, who was the Director of the CIA at the time, conceded, "The use of homosexuals as a control mechanism over individuals recruited for espionage is a generally accepted technique which has been used at least on a limited basis for many years. While this agency will never employ homosexuals on its rolls, it might conceivably be necessary, and in the past has actually been valuable, to use known homosexuals as agents in the field. I am certain that if Josef Stalin or a member of the Politburo or a high satellite official were known to be a homosexual, no member of this committee or of the Congress would balk against our use of any technique to penetrate their operations...after all, intelligence and espionage is, at best, an extremely dirty business."

Though McCarthy's work appealed to many Americans, others were worried by the direction they saw him going. *The Washington Post* began to refer to his quest as "McCarthyism," a name that has stuck for over 60 years, but instead of trying to run from the term, McCarthy embraced it, famously saying, "McCarthyism is Americanism with its sleeves rolled."

McCarthy also wasted no time in going after his political enemies, starting with his personal campaign against Tydings in the latter's 1950 bid for reelection. While campaigning on behalf of Tydings' opponent, McCarthy went so far as to imply that Tydings himself had communist leanings. Tydings ultimately lost the race, and several men McCarthy campaigned for won their bids for office. This elevated his status among Republicans, many of whom had to admit that, whether they liked him or not, his favor was a huge political asset that helped lead to Republican gains in the 1950 midterms.

Naturally, McCarthy basked in the glow of his influence. In *McCarthyism: The Fight for America*, he thundered that "stupidity and eagerness to keep a corrupt party at the public trough can destroy a nation as effectively and as quickly as treason — especially when traitors can use men of little minds who put party above country. There is no secret about the fact that 10 of those whom I named before the Tydings Committee have either been convicted or removed from the State Department under the loyalty program. Neither is there any secret about the fact that my exposure of the Truman Administration's whitewash and cover-up of Communist traitors in government has awakened and sickened the American people to the extent that a change in administration — either to a decent Democrat or Republican— is inevitable..."

Of course, there were many in public office who considered McCarthy dangerous, both politically and morally. Among them was Harry Truman, whom McCarthy often accused of being soft on Communism. McCarthy both despised and feared the president: "From the day Truman announced on February 23, 1950, that he would do everything in his power to 'disprove McCarthy's charges,' the Administration has used all of its power — all of its publicity agents paid for by the taxpayers — to clear men like Lattimore, Davies, Vincent and Acheson, and to attempt to discredit and smear McCarthy. ... As early as April, 1950, President Truman called to the White House for a conference William Evjue, editor of the Madison Capital Times, a man who, as previously stated, maintains on his staff as city editor, Cedric Parker, who Evjue himself in an editorial called 'the Communist leader in Madison.' At the conclusion of the White House conference, Evjue announced to the press that the President assured him the Administration would continue to fight McCarthyism."

McCarthy also went after General George Marshall, the former Army Chief of Staff, former Secretary of State and coordinator of the Marshall Plan that helped get Europe back on its feet. McCarthy despised the general and even published a book about his supposed exploits. He concluded 1951's *America's Retreat From Victory: The Story Of George Catlett Marshall* by writing, "If Marshall were merely stupid, the laws of probability would have dictated that at least some of his decisions would have served this country's interest. Even if Marshall had been innocent of guilty intention, how could he have been trusted to guide the defense of this country further? We have declined so precipitously in relation to the Soviet Union in the last six years, how much swifter may be our fall into disaster with Marshall's policies continuing to guide us? Where will all this stop? This is not a rhetorical question; ours is not a rhetorical danger. Where next will Marshall's policies, continued by Acheson, carry us? What is the objective of the conspiracy? I think it is clear from what has occurred and is now occurring: to diminish the United States in world affairs, to weaken us militarily, to confuse our spirit with talk of surrender in the Far East and to impair our will to resist evil. To what end? To the end that we shall be contained and frustrated and finally fall victim to Soviet intrigue from within and Russian military might from without. Is that far-fetched? There have been many examples in history of rich and powerful states which have been corrupted from within, enfeebled and deceived until they were unable to resist aggression."

Marshall

Furthermore, McCarthy supported General Douglas MacArthur, whom Truman also despised. McCarthy considered MacArthur a fellow martyr in the war against communism, writing, "The third group, and of course the loudest, was made up of the official Communist papers such as the Daily Worker, which bitterly condemned McCarthy in a stream of editorials and colorfully lauded General Marshall as a 'great hero.' A few days after the Marshall speech the Daily Worker denounced General MacArthur and myself as the 'two most vociferous architects of fascist propaganda.' 'An integral part of the technique,' wrote the Communist Daily Worker in referring to the 'fascism' of General MacArthur and myself, 'is the gutter insult hurled at individuals such as Truman, Acheson and Marshall, whose high positions, irrespective of their character, would in ordinary times protect them from personal attacks of this sort.'"

MacArthur

When analyzing McCarthy's fight against communism, it is important to note that it was not divided exclusively along party lines. There were a number of Republicans who opposed him and a number of Democrats who supported him. Chief among the latter was the rising Kennedy family; like McCarthy, they were Catholics, a strongly anti-communist faction in the United States at that time. In June 1950, the *Brooklyn Tablet*, a Catholic newspaper, demanded that its readers "[p]ut up or shut up:" "The time for being naive about the substance of the McCarthy charges is long past. The presence of close to a hundred perverts in the State Department—even though [Alger] Hiss has been forced out and convicted and the perverts fired—justify [sic] a complete and thorough search for further evidences of the Communist conspiracy within the departments of our government. That is the avowed objective of Senator McCarthy's efforts. … It is time to put the direct question to each Congressman and Senator: 'What are YOU doing about getting rid of Communists in our government? It is YOUR job as well as Senator McCarthy's. What are YOU doing about it? … It is time for every Congressman and Senator to put up or shut up. If he (or she) cannot offer any better way of reaching and destroying the Communist conspiracy in our government than is being offered by Senator McCarthy, then at least, for the welfare of the United States, let him hold his peace and be silent!"

Not only was McCarthy friendly with "Old Man Joe" Kennedy, he even dated two of his daughters. McCarthy was especially close to Robert Kennedy, who served on his investigating committee for a short time, and he was even the godfather of Bobby's first child. As a freshman Senator, John F. Kennedy refused to join his fellow Democrats in attacking McCarthy, explaining to Arthur Schlesinger, "Hell, half my voters in Massachusetts look on McCarthy as a hero."

McCarthy and Bobby Kennedy

McCarthy proved to be something of a thorn in the side of Dwight Eisenhower when the latter was campaigning for president in 1952. Ike had to be close enough to the Senator to carry Wisconsin but at the same time not so close as to be tainted by his radical ideas. Once in office, Eisenhower worked against him behind the scenes, but he remained reluctant to challenge McCarthy publicly. As he candidly wrote in a private letter in 1953, "I really believe that nothing will be so effective in combating his particular kind of troublemaking as to ignore him. This he cannot stand."

Eisenhower

McCarthy himself had also won re-election in 1952 handily, though he had not done as well as many other Republicans in Wisconsin. For his part, he seemed to feel no sense of party loyalty and remained critical of Eisenhower until his death.

AMERICANS.....

DON'T PATRONIZE REDS !!!!

YOU CAN DRIVE THE REDS OUT OF TELEVISION, RADIO AND HOLLYWOOD.....

THIS TRACT WILL TELL YOU HOW.

WHY WE MUST DRIVE THEM OUT:

1) The REDS have made our Screen, Radio and TV Moscow's most effective Fifth Column in America . . . 2) The REDS of Hollywood and Broadway have always been the chief financial support of Communist propaganda in America . . . 3) OUR OWN FILMS, made by RED Producers, Directors, Writers and STARS, are being used by Moscow in ASIA, Africa, the Balkans and throughout Europe to create hatred of America . . . 4) RIGHT NOW films are being made to craftily glorify MARXISM, UNESCO and ONE-WORLDISM . . . and via your TV Set they are being piped into your Living Room—and are poisoning the minds of your children under your very eyes ! ! !

So REMEMBER — If you patronize a Film made by RED Producers, Writers, Stars and STUDIOS you are aiding and abetting COMMUNISM . . . every time you permit REDS to come into your Living Room VIA YOUR TV SET you are helping MOSCOW and the INTERNATIONALISTS to destroy America ! ! !

Anti-Communist literature from the 1950s

"It is clear that much of our failure in international affairs was due to incompetence, the inability of our leaders to understand or to cope with the major problems which confronted us. But it also becomes increasingly clear that our failures were aggravated by the fact that disloyal elements had infiltrated into several of our government agencies. The number of actively disloyal persons was comparatively small, but they were able to do an enormous amount of damage. In 1945 much of our power and prestige was due to the fact that we alone were possessors of the secret of the atomic bomb. It has now been clearly proved that several American citizens, working in connection with various atomic energy projects, gave or sold extremely important items of information to the Soviet authorities. This is undoubtedly one of the reasons why the USSR has made such rapid strides in developing its own atomic bomb. It has also been clearly proved that several persons occupying high and responsible positions in the government were, at one time or another, active members of Communist cells, and that such persons perjured themselves when they denied this fact." – Joseph McCarthy, *McCarthyism: The Fight for America* (1952)

In 1953, McCarthy became Chairman of the Senate Committee on Government Operations, a position he was given in the hopes that it would keep him out of trouble. However, those in charge miscalculated, because McCarthy soon found a way to use the Senate Permanent Subcommittee on Investigations, also under his purview, to continue to weed out government workers he suspected of being Communists. He had a strong staff working for him, with Roy Cohn serving as his chief counsel and young Bobby Kennedy working as Cohn's assistant. McCarthy's work on the subcommittee was the high point of his career to date, and it proved to be the pinnacle from which he fell so quickly and so far.

Cohn

From his new position, McCarthy began by going after Voice of America, radio broadcasts produced by the State Department in part to counter Soviet propaganda around the world. Ironically, McCarthy accused the VOA of publishing articles of known Communists. While questioning Ed Kretzmann, one of the VOA's policy advisors, McCarthy mentioned a memo circulated within the office: "The only way you can interpret this, if it needs interpretation, is that [it] is saying, 'If you find a man like [Howard] Fast, who has a reputation of being a Communist, you can use him if you find something in his writings which you think should be used.' That is, in effect, what he says? ... There is nothing here that indicates that you are asking for comments on what is entitled 'Information Policy for Use of Materials Produced by Controversial Persons.' Would it not be proper for me to assume, if I were head of one of the desks over in the Voice, and I received this that I could consider this as the policy? ... It would seem, offhand, this would be very unwise and that it would give them stature as being recognized by the Voice as authorities and would give their works wider publication."

Kretzmann subsequently called this investigation the VOA's "darkest hour," complaining that "Senator McCarthy and his chief hatchet man, Roy Cohn, almost succeeded in muffling it." The situation might have been much worse had President Eisenhower not spoken out against McCarthy's censorship efforts, telling a group of students at Dartmouth University, "Don't join the book burners. Don't think you are going to conceal faults by concealing evidence that they ever existed. Don't be afraid to go into your library and read every book as long as any document does not offend our own ideas of decency. That should be the only censorship. How will we defeat Communism unless we know what it is? ...Now we have got to fight it with something better. Not try to conceal the thinking of our own people."

After his attack on the Voice of America produced little except headlines for the Senator, there came an incident that indicated McCarthy was beginning to push his battle against Communist subversion too far. Once he was chair of the Subcommittee on Investigations, McCarthy chose J.B. Matthews to be his staff director. Matthews' credentials for the job were impeccable, as he had previously been the staff director for the House Un-American Activities Committee, but problems arose due to an article Matthews had written called "Reds and Our Churches." It opened with the shocking declaration that the "largest single group supporting the Communist apparatus in the United States today is composed of Protestant clergymen." It then went on to charge, "Since the beginning of the First Cold War in April, 1948, the Communist Party of this country has placed more and more reliance upon the ranks of the Protestant clergy to provide the party's subversive apparatus with its agents, stooges, dupes, front men, and fellow-travelers. Clergymen outnumber professors two to one in supporting the Communist-front apparatus of the Kremlin conspiracy. ...during the past seventeen years the Communist Party has enlisted the support of at least thirty-five hundred professors — many of them as dues-paying members, many others as fellow-travelers, some as out-and-out espionage agents, some as adherents of the party line in varying degrees, and some as the unwitting dupes of subversion. During the same seventeen-year period, the Communist Party has enlisted the support of at least seven thousand Protestant clergymen in the same categories — party members, fellow-travelers, espionage agents, party-line adherents, and unwitting dupes."

Matthews

Needless to say, this article did not go over well in the predominantly Protestant America of the 1950s, even among fellow anticommunists, and McCarthy was forced to dismiss Matthews. This was the first time he had ever felt compelled to back down, and it proved to be the beginning of the end for him.

Chapter 6: Guilty of Hoodwinking the American Public

"Of even greater importance and significance was a group of 'fellow travellers,' persons who never joined the Communist party, persons who are horrified when accused of treason or disloyalty, but who joyfully followed the Communist party line in their advocacy or rejection of causes and policies. A person may agree with the Communist position on one or two points, even on three or four, without necessarily coming under suspicion. But when a person, during the course of several years, always speaks and writes in favor of ideas which closely parallel the policies advanced by the Communist hierarchy, it would appear obvious that either his intelligence or his integrity as an American citizen is open to doubt. Such persons are unworthy of being considered 'experts,' as they often claim to be, or else are guilty of hoodwinking the American public as to what is going on in national and international affairs. I do not believe that such persons should be persecuted, but I do believe that such persons should be eliminated from positions where they are able to influence national policy." – Joseph McCarthy, *McCarthyism: The Fight for America* (1952)

McCarthy followed the Matthews' blunder with a bigger one by choosing to go after the United States Army. This proved to be a much more formidable foe than the State Department, and one that proved to be his undoing.

Part of McCarthy's problem was that his search for subversives in the Army lacked the support of the public. The American people had little direct contact with the State Department, unless they applied for a passport, so they could more easily believe that it was riddled with highly educated Communists who did not have their best interest at heart. The Army was another story, as most American families either had or knew someone who served in World War II or were then fighting in Korea; the idea that there were subversive elements in the Army was much harder to believe.

McCarthy began by cutting short his own honeymoon (he had recently married Jean Kerr) to lead the investigation of the Army Signal Corps Lab at Fort Monmouth. It proved to be a fruitless endeavor, as McCarthy's committee was unable to find any evidence that the Signal Corps had been infiltrated by Communists. Next, McCarthy went after Irving Peress, an Army Major who proved to be a member of the American Labor Party. McCarthy subpoenaed Peress, who appeared before the committee but refused to answer any questions, citing his Fifth Amendment right to not incriminate himself. McCarthy then contacted Robert Stevens, the Secretary of the Army, and insisted that Peress be court-martialed, but instead, Brigadier General Ralph Zwicker went ahead and approved Peress' pending honorable discharge.

Peress

Zwicker

Stevens

McCarthy subsequently called Colonel Chester T. Brown before the committee, during which the following exchange took place.

> McCarthy: Let's say you have investigated, now, and the investigation has ended. The investigation shows that Colonel Jones knew that Captain Peress had refused to answer questions about his communist activities, invoking the Fifth Amendment and thereafter Colonel Jones approved this man's promotion to major. Would you say Colonel Jones should be removed from the military? Let's assume all of those facts are proven positively.

> Brown: I don't consider myself qualified to state an opinion on that, sir.

McCarthy: You are ordered to. Being a servant of the people, sir, like I am, we are entitled to know how you are handling your job. One way to find out is to know how you feel about these Communists, especially when you, yourself, were part and parcel of the organization that kept on a traitor. So you are ordered to answer that question.

Brown: I would say, sir, that some disciplinary action should be taken.

Believing he had drawn blood, McCarthy initiated the following exchange:

McCarthy: I said let us assume that Colonel Jones knew that Captain Peress had refused to answer questions about Communist activities and membership in his party, and Colonel Jones thereafter approved the promotion of Captain Peress to major. Would you say Colonel Jones should be retained in our military?

Brown: No, sir.

McCarthy: Let us go a step further. Let us assume that Colonel or General Jones is aware of the fact that Major Peress has been before this committee, has been identified as a Communist, has been identified as having attended Communist leadership schools, that his wife has been identified as a Communist, and that Peress refuses to answer any questions asked him by this committee about Communist activity on the grounds of self-incrimination. Then, say, subsequent to that McCarthy of the committee writes a letter to the secretary of the army urging a court-martial of Major Peress, and that the day after that letter is made public, Colonel Jones signs an honorable discharge for this man, knowing all the facts which I have just related. Would you say that Colonel Jones should be removed from the army?

Brown: Not necessarily, sir, because Colonel Jones would only give an honorable discharge upon a direction from higher authority.

McCarthy: Well, how about the higher authority, then? Do you think he should be removed from the army, assuming he knows those facts?

Brown: If the higher authority knew all the facts, yes, sir; I think he should.

McCarthy: You think he should be removed?

Brown: Yes, sir.

Finally, he moved in for the kill.

McCarthy: Do you think that a committee should be able to get the information as to who is responsible for the promotion, and the honorable discharge of this man, or do you think that would endanger the national security if we got that information?

Brown: Simply as my personal opinion, as one of the Indians on the lower level, I think the committee might well be given the facts by the proper authorities.

McCarthy: Do you know who is responsible for the ordering of the honorable discharge for Major Peress?

Brown: I don't know the name of any individual, no, sir.

McCarthy: Have you not discussed that since he got this honorable discharge?

Brown: No, sir. The directive came from the Department of the Army. It was not questioned at our headquarters.

McCarthy: Who signed that order?

Since he never got a straight answer, McCarthy made "Who promoted Peress?" a popular catch phrase among his supporters. What he didn't reveal was that Peress, a dentist, was automatically promoted because of the Doctor Draft Act, an initiative McCarthy had actually voted for himself.

McCarthy and Cohn during the McCarthy-Army Hearings

In going after the army, McCarthy finally overstepped his bounds, and in the early months of

1954, the Army struck back. It accused McCarthy and Cohn of putting undue pressure on the Army to promote David Schine, a mutual friend and former aide who had been drafted. The Senate Permanent Subcommittee on Investigations was called on to investigate, and Karl Mundt was given McCarthy's own position as chair for the duration of the hearings, which began on April 22, 1954.

A picture of Schine during testimony

Mundt

The hearings were televised so all of America could watch, and Secretary Robert Stevens came out fighting: "Gentlemen of the committee, I am here today at the request of this committee. You have my assurance of the fullest cooperation. In order that we may all be quite clear as to just why this hearing has come about, it is necessary for me to refer at the outset to Pvt. G. David Schine, a former consultant of this committee. David Schine was eligible for the draft. Efforts were made by McCarthy of this committee, Senator Joseph R. McCarthy, and the subcommittee's chief counsel, Mr. Roy M. Cohn, to secure a commission for him. Mr. Schine was not qualified, and he was not commissioned. Selective Service then drafted him. Subsequent efforts were made to seek preferential treatment for him after he was inducted. Before getting into the Schine story I want to make two general comments. First, it is my responsibility to speak for the Army. The Army is about a million and a half men and women, in posts across this country and around the world, on active duty and in the National Guard and Organized Reserves, plus hundreds of thousands of loyal and faithful civil servants."

At this point, McCarthy rose to challenge him, insisting, "Mr. Stevens is not speaking for the Army. He is speaking for Mr. Stevens, for Mr. [John G.] Adams, and Mr. [H. Struve] Hensel. The committee did not make the Army a party to this controversy, and I think it is highly improper to try to make the Army a party. Mr. Stevens can only speak for himself. ... All we were investigating has been some Communists in the Army, a very small percentage, I would say much less than 1 percent. And when the Secretary says that, in effect 'I am speaking for the Army,' he is putting the 99.9 percent of good, honorable, loyal men in the Army into the position of trying to oppose the exposure of Communists in the Army. I think it should be made clear at the outset, so we need not waste time on it, hour after hour, that Mr. Stevens is speaking for Mr. Stevens and those who are speaking through him; when Mr. Adams speaks, he is speaking for Mr. Adams and those who are speaking through him, and likewise Mr. Hensel. I may say I resent very, very much this attempt to connect the great American Army with this attempt to sabotage the efforts of this committee's investigation into communism...."

Counselor for the Army John G. Adams later rose to give his recollection of the Schine incident, telling the committee, "I wanted Senator McCarthy to restate before Mr. Cohn what he had told me on the courthouse steps, I said, 'Let's talk about Schine.' That started a chain of events, an experience similar to none which I have had in my life. Mr. Cohn became extremely agitated, became extremely abusive. ... I was trying to catch a 1:30 train, but Mr. Cohn was so violent by then that I felt I had better not do it and leave him that angry with me and that angry with Senator McCarthy because of a remark I had made. ...the thing that he was so violent about, was the fact that, (1), the Army was not agreeing to an assignment for Schine and, (2), that Senator McCarthy was not supporting his staff in its efforts to get Schine assigned to New York. So his abuse was directed partly to me and partly to Senator McCarthy. ... At first Senator McCarthy seemed to be trying to conciliate. He seemed to be trying to conciliate Cohn and not to state anything contrary to what he had stated to me in the morning. But then he more or less lapsed into silence...."

Adams then went on to describe what happened later, when they talked again of Schine: "I asked him what would happen if Schine got overseas duty. ... He responded with vigor and force, 'Stevens is through as Secretary of the Army.' I said, 'Oh, Roy,' something to this effect, 'Oh, Roy, don't say that. Come on. Really, what is going to happen if Schine gets overseas duty?' He responded with even more force, 'We will wreck the Army.' Then he said, 'The first thing we are going to do is get General Ryan for the way he has treated Dave at Fort Dix. Dave gets through at Fort Dix tomorrow or this week, and as soon as he is gone we are going to get General Ryan for the obscene way in which he has permitted Schine to be treated up there.' He said, 'We are not going to do it ourselves. We have another committee of the Congress interested in it.' Then he said, 'I wouldn't put it past you to do this. We will start investigations. We have enough stuff on the Army to keep investigations going indefinitely, and if anything like such-and-such doublecross occurs, that is what we will do.' This remark was not to be taken lightly in the context in which it was given to me...."

Not surprisingly, Cohn denied making such statements: "I am sure I did not make that statement, and I am sure that Mr. Adams and anybody else with any sense, and Mr. Adams has a lot of sense, could ever believe that I was threatening to wreck the Army or that I could wreck the Army. I say, sir, that the statement is ridiculous."

The hearings got further out of control when McCarthy rose to attack the Army's Chief Counsel, Joseph Welch, whom he felt had been attacking Cohn. "I thought we should just call to your attention the fact that your Mr. Fisher [Fred Fisher, a junior attorney at Welch's law firm], who is still in your law firm today, whom you asked to have down here looking over the secret and classified material, is a member of an organization, not named by me but named by various committees, named by the Attorney General, as I recall, and I think I quote this verbatim, as 'the legal bulwark of the Communist Party.' He belonged to that for a sizable number of years, according to his own admission, and he belonged to it long after it had been exposed as the legal arm of the Communist Party. … I am not asking you at this time to explain why you tried to foist him on this committee. Whether you knew he was a member of that Communist organization or not, I don't know. I assume you did not, Mr. Welch, because I get the impression that, while you are quite an actor, you play for a laugh, I don't think you have any conception of the danger of the Communist Party. I don't think you yourself would ever knowingly aid the Communist cause. I think you are unknowingly aiding it when you try to burlesque this hearing in which we are attempting to bring out the facts, however."

Much to the delight of some and the embarrassment of others, the most memorable part of the hearings was Welch's response: "Until this moment, Senator, I think I never really gauged your cruelty or your recklessness. Fred Fisher is a young man who went to the Harvard Law School and came into my firm and is starting what looks to be a brilliant career with us…When I decided to work for this committee I asked Jim St. Clair, who sits on my right, to be my first assistant. I said to Jim, 'Pick somebody in the firm who works under you that you would like.' … I then said to these two young men, 'Boys…if there is anything funny in the life of either one of you that would hurt anybody in this case you speak up quick.' Fred Fisher said, 'Mr. Welch, when I was in law school and for a period of months after, I belonged to the Lawyers Guild….' I said, 'Fred, I just don't think I am going to ask you to work on the case. If I do, one of these days that will come out and go over national television and it will just hurt like the dickens'. …I fear he shall always bear a scar needlessly inflicted by you. If it were in my power to forgive you for your reckless cruelty, I will do so. I like to think I am a gentleman, but your forgiveness will have to come from someone other than me…Let us not assassinate this lad further, Senator. You have done enough. Have you no sense of decency sir, at long last? Have you left no sense of decency?"

After hearing from a total of 32 witnesses, the committee concluded that while McCarthy had not done anything wrong, Cohn had tried to influence the Army through "unduly persistent or aggressive efforts" on Schine's behalf.

A picture of McCarthy questioning Welch

Chapter 7: Bleed Them

"Here we see 'honest,' 'upright,' 'virtuous' Democrat 'statesmen' 'protecting' America and 'fearlessly ' and 'bravely' 'fighting' Communism. If the committee is trying to prove that I am guilty of the crime of not being wealthy, I must plead guilty. The money I have spent hiring investigators and paying their traveling expenses to dig out the evidence on Communists has, of course, not improved my financial condition. Then also there are the very heavy legal and investigators' fees which I have had to pay in connection with the lawsuits which have resulted from this Communist fight. According to Louis Budenz, former member of the Communist Party's National Committee, and editor of the Daily Worker, the strategy of the Communist Party is to force into lawsuits anyone who dares expose Communists, and thus through the payment of attorney's fees bleed them financially white. If I were on the other side of the fight, protecting Communists, unlimited legal services would have been offered to me and there would be no objection by Benton and no investigation by the Gillette-Monroney-Hennings Committee." – Joseph McCarthy, *McCarthyism: The Fight for America* (1952)

While Welch embarrassed McCarthy during the hearings, another blow to McCarthy's career also came during the hearings when Edward R. Murrow took aim at him during the March 9, 1954 episode of his popular CBS series *See It Now*. After showing a number of clips of McCarthy badgering different people and making outrageous speeches, Murrow concluded his broadcast with these words: "No one familiar with the history of this country can deny that congressional committees are useful. It is necessary to investigate before legislating, but the line between investigating and persecuting is a very fine one, and the junior Senator from Wisconsin has stepped over it repeatedly. His primary achievement has been in confusing the public mind, as between the internal and the external threats of Communism. We must not confuse dissent with disloyalty. We must remember always that accusation is not proof and that conviction depends upon evidence and due process of law. We will not walk in fear, one of another. We will not be driven by fear into an age of unreason, if we dig deep in our history and our doctrine, and remember that we are not descended from fearful men—not from men who feared to write, to speak, to associate and to defend causes that were, for the moment, unpopular. This is no time for men who oppose Senator McCarthy's methods to keep silent, or for those who approve. We can deny our heritage and our history, but we cannot escape responsibility for the result. There is no way for a citizen of a republic to abdicate his responsibilities. As a nation we have come into our full inheritance at a tender age. We proclaim ourselves, as indeed we are, the defenders of freedom, wherever it continues to exist in the world, but we cannot defend freedom abroad by deserting it at home. The actions of the junior Senator from Wisconsin have caused alarm and dismay amongst our allies abroad, and given considerable comfort to our enemies. And whose fault is that? Not really his. He didn't create this situation of fear; he merely exploited it—and rather successfully. Cassius was right: 'The fault, dear Brutus, is not in our stars, but in ourselves.'"

Murrow

Murrow followed up his first attack on McCarthy with another *See It Now* episode, this one dedicated to defending Annie Lee Moss, an African-American woman working as an Army clerk. McCarthy had earlier accused her of being a Communist but had not perused the matter very far. Writing about Moss and her testimony, Ethel Payne, a journalist with the African-American paper *Chicago Defender* during the 1950s, recalled, "Now, Annie Lee Moss was a file clerk, and she worked in the Pentagon basement. It was her duty to carry…the tapes and things back, when they were used, to carry and put them in their proper place. She handled just routine messages. She never really came in contact with any sensitive material. … In those days, when the Communist Party was really campaigning in black areas to recruit blacks to join the Communist Party, they were very active. … Well, Mrs. Moss' husband was one of those who had been contacted by the communists. He was just a simple working man, but they were sending him free subscriptions to the Daily Worker, the organ of the Communist Party. And I don't know what he did with them, but when he died, they kept coming, these papers, and they piled up on her back porch, some with the wrappings still on them. … And so she didn't pay any attention to it, but somehow, somebody, some informant, told them that she was getting the Daily Worker. So triumphantly, McCarthy produces this "star witness," as evidence of communism, and he claimed that she was a card-carrying member of the Communist Party — all of this was fabricated by Roy Cohn."

After noting that Moss' attorney was not allowed to speak on her behalf, Payne continued, "And she turned, in bewilderment, to her lawyer. The mike was open, and she said 'Who is Karl Marx? Who is Karl Marx?' Well, the fact that she put it in the present tense — she didn't say, 'Who was Karl Marx.' She said, 'Who is Karl Marx?' Well, you know, to the press, this was dynamite, you know. This was a real story. Here's this poor woman who was being pilloried as a Communist front agent and all this, and she asks, 'Who is Karl Marx?' meaning she didn't know what was going on, she didn't know who Karl Marx was or anything, and that she put in the present tense meant that she was totally innocent. So in a mad dash, they were rushing out of the newsroom to put this on the wire, telephone it in and everything, and the hearing room just exploded in laughter. Of course, all this was terribly embarrassing to McCarthy, and he became quite angry…"

Annie Lee Moss

McCarthy soon made another fatal mistake when he agreed to be interviewed by Murrow for the April 6 episode of *See It Now*. Murrow himself edited the film in such a way as to make McCarthy look as bad as possible. Even John Cogley, a journalist who had long criticized McCarthy, observed, "A totally different selection of film would turn McCarthy into a man on a shining white steed -- infinitely reasonable, burdened with the onus of single-handedly cleaning out subversives in the face of violent criticism. ... Combined with selectivity [television] would explode in any person's or any group's face."

In the midst of these events, the *Sauk-Prairie Star* of Sauk City, Wisconsin began campaigning to have McCarthy recalled. Editor Leroy Gore led the charge for recall, calling the effort the "Joe Must Go" campaign. In spite of his best efforts, and those of many others, the committee failed to receive the more than 400,000 signatures required to put the recall to a vote, but even still, the die was cast: Tail-Gunner Joe was on his way out.

Many Senators had wanted for some time to get rid of McCarthy, and Wisconsin's recall threat, coupled with the other issues over the past few months, gave them the excuse they needed to proceed. Ralph Flanders, a Republican Senator from Vermont, ignited the flame when he condemned McCarthy in a March 9, 1954 speech before the Senate: "I have never seen nor heard anything to match the dust and racket of this particular job of housecleaning. Is the necessary housecleaning the great task before the United States, or do we face far more dangerous problems? If he cannot view the larger scene and the real danger, let him return to his housecleaning. But let him not so work as to conceal mortal danger in which our country finds itself from the external enemies of mankind."

Flanders

Several weeks later, Flanders proposed that McCarthy be censured on 46 counts, and Senator Arthur Watkins of Utah was tapped to form a committee to consider the question. The committee began hearings on August 31, and after two months, it returned its decision that of the 46 counts against him, only two were actionable. On December 2, they concluded:

> "Resolved, That the Senator from Wisconsin, Mr. McCarthy, failed to cooperate with the Subcommittee on Privileges and Elections of the Senate Committee on Rules and Administration in clearing up matters referred to that subcommittee which concerned his conduct as a Senator and affected the honor of the Senate and, instead, repeatedly abused the subcommittee and its members who were trying to carry out assigned duties, thereby obstructing the constitutional processes of the Senate, and that this conduct of the Senator from Wisconsin, Mr. McCarthy, is contrary to senatorial traditions and is hereby condemned.
>
> Sec 2. The Senator from Wisconsin, Mr. McCarthy, in writing to the Chairman of the Select Committee to Study Censure Charges (Mr. Watkins) after the Select Committee had issued its report and before the report was presented to the Senate

charging three members of the Select Committee with 'deliberate deception' and 'fraud' for failure to disqualify themselves; in stating to the press on November 4, 1954, that the special Senate session that was to begin November 8, 1954, was a 'lynch-party'; in repeatedly describing this special Senate session as a 'lynch bee' in a nationwide television and radio show on November 7, 1954; in stating to the public press on November 13, 1954, that McCarthy of the Select Committee (Mr. Watkins) was guilty of 'the most unusual, most cowardly things I've ever heard of' and stating further: 'I expected he would be afraid to answer the questions, but didn't think he'd be stupid enough to make a public statement'; and in characterizing the said committee as the 'unwitting handmaiden,' 'involuntary agent' and 'attorneys-in-fact' of the Communist Party and in charging that the said committee in writing its report 'imitated Communist methods -- that it distorted, misrepresented, and omitted in its effort to manufacture a plausible rationalization' in support of its recommendations to the Senate, which characterizations and charges were contained in a statement released to the press and inserted in the Congressional Record of November 10, 1954, acted contrary to senatorial ethics and tended to bring the Senate into dishonor and disrepute, to obstruct the constitutional processes of the Senate, and to impair its dignity; and such conduct is hereby condemned."

Watkins

On December 2, 1954, the Senate passed the Committee's motion to censure McCarthy on both counts by a vote of 67 to 22. With that, McCarthy's career was over for all intents and purposes. He served out the remainder of his Senate term in disgrace, largely ignored by those around him, but at the same time, Brent Bozell, who worked as an aide for him during that period, later claimed, "To insist, as some have, that McCarthy was a shattered man after the censure is sheer nonsense. His intellect was as sharp as ever. When he addressed himself to a problem, he was perfectly capable of dealing with it." McCarthy also continued to work against any sort of cooperation with Communist countries, saying, "You cannot offer friendship to tyrants and murderers ... without advancing the cause of tyranny and murder." On another occasion, he said, "Coexistence with Communists is neither possible nor honorable nor desirable. Our long term objective must be the eradication of Communism from the face of the earth."

As it turned out, McCarthy's body was not able to keep up with his spirit, owing primarily to his advanced alcoholism. Richard Rovere, a popular journalist of the time, noted, "He had always been a heavy drinker, and there were times in those seasons of discontent when he drank more than ever. But he was not always drunk. He went on the wagon (for him this meant beer instead of whiskey) for days and weeks at a time. The difficulty toward the end was that he couldn't hold the stuff. He went to pieces on his second or third drink. And he did not snap back quickly."

Joe McCarthy's alcoholism finally took his life on May 2, 1957. He was just 48 years old. 70 of his fellow Senators attended his Requiem Mass at St. Matthew's Cathedral in Washington, the same Cathedral that, just a few short years later, would be the scene of the slain President John F. Kennedy's Requiem Mass.

Online Resources

Other books about Cold War history by Charles River Editors

Other books about 20th century American history by Charles River Editors

Other books about Joseph McCarthy on Amazon

Bibliography

Anderson, Jack and May, Ronald W (1952). McCarthy: the man, the Senator, the "ism," Beacon Press.

Bayley, Edwin R. (1981). Joe McCarthy and the Press. University of Wisconsin Press. ISBN 0-299-08624-0.

Belfrage, Cedric (1989). The American Inquisition, 1945–1960: A Profile of the "McCarthy Era". Thunder's Mouth Press. ISBN 0-938410-87-3.

Buckley, William F. (1954). McCarthy and His Enemies: The Record and Its Meaning. Regnery Publishing. ISBN 0-89526-472-2.

Cook, Fred J. (1971). The Nightmare Decade: The Life and Times of Senator Joe McCarthy. Random House. ISBN 0-394-46270-X.

Crosby, Donald F. (1978). God, Church, and Flag: Senator Joseph R. McCarthy and the Catholic Church, 1950–1957. University of North Carolina Press. ISBN 0-8078-1312-5.

Evans, M. Stanton (2007). Blacklisted By History: The Real Story of Joseph McCarthy and His Fight Against America's Enemies. Crown Forum. ISBN 1-4000-8105-X.

Freeland, Richard M. (1985). The Truman Doctrine and the Origins of McCarthyism: Foreign Policy, Domestic Politics, and Internal Security, 1946–1948. New York University Press. ISBN 0-8147-2576-7.

Fried, Richard M. (1977). Men Against McCarthy. Columbia University Press. ISBN 0-231-08360-2.

Fried, Richard M. (1990). Nightmare in Red: The McCarthy Era in Perspective. Oxford University Press. ISBN 0-19-504361-8.

Griffith, Robert (1970). The Politics of Fear: Joseph R. McCarthy and the Senate. University of Massachusetts Press. ISBN 0-87023-555-9.

Herman, Arthur (1999). Joseph McCarthy: Reexamining the Life and Legacy of America's Most Hated Senator. Free Press. ISBN 0-684-83625-4.

Latham, Earl (1969). Communist Controversy in Washington: From the New Deal to McCarthy. Macmillan Publishing Company. ISBN 0-689-70121-7.

O'Brien, Michael (1981). McCarthy and McCarthyism in Wisconsin. Olympic Marketing Corp. ISBN 0-8262-0319-1.

Oshinsky, David M. (2005) [1983]. A Conspiracy So Immense: The World of Joe McCarthy. Oxford University Press. ISBN 0-19-515424-X.

Powers, Richard Gid (1997). Not Without Honor: A History of American AntiCommunism. Free Press. ISBN 0-300-07470-0.

Ranville, Michael (1996). To Strike at a King: The Turning Point in the McCarthy Witch-Hunt. Momentum Books Limited. ISBN 1-879094-53-3.

Reeves, Thomas C. (1982). The Life and Times of Joe McCarthy: A Biography. Madison

Books. ISBN 1-56833-101-0.

Rovere, Richard H. (1959). Senator Joe McCarthy. University of California Press. ISBN 0-520-20472-7.

Schrecker, Ellen (1998). Many Are the Crimes: McCarthyism in America. Little, Brown. ISBN 0-316-77470-7.

Strout, Lawrence N. (1999). Covering McCarthyism: How the Christian Science Monitor Handled Joseph R. McCarthy, 1950–1954. Greenwood Press. ISBN 0-313-31091-2.

Wicker, Tom (2006). Shooting Star: The Brief Arc of Joe McCarthy. Harcourt. ISBN 0-15-101082-X.

Made in the USA
Columbia, SC
26 March 2020